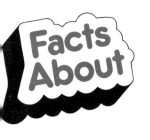
Facts About

Fish

DONNA BAILEY

STECK-VAUGHN
L I B R A R Y
Austin, Texas

How to Use This Book

This book tells you many things about fish. There is a Table of Contents on the next page. It shows you what each double page of the book is about. For example, pages 26 and 27 tell you about ''Bony Fish.''

On most of these pages you will find some words that are printed in **bold** type. The bold type shows you that these words are in the glossary on pages 46 and 47. The glossary explains the meaning of some words that may be new to you.

At the very end of the book there is an index. The index tells you where to find certain words in the book. For example, you can use it to look up words like camouflage, barbel, gill, and many other words to do with fish.

Published in the United States in 1990 by Steck-Vaughn Co., Austin, Texas, a subsidiary of National Education Corporation.

© Macmillan Children's Books 1988
Artwork © BLA Publishing Limited 1988

Material used in this book first appeared in Macmillan World Library: *Life In The Water.* Published by Macmillan Children's Books

Designed by Julian Holland

Printed and bound in the United States

1 2 3 4 5 6 7 8 9 0 LB 94 93 92 91 90

Library of Congress Cataloging-in-Publication Data

Bailey, Donna.
  Fish/ Donna Bailey.
    p.   cm. — (Facts about)
  Summary: Text and illustrations introduce sea animals from the simplest types such as corals and sponges to the more highly developed fish and sharks.
  ISBN 0-8114-2508-8
  1. Fishes—Juvenile literature.   2. Marine invertebrates—Juvenile literature. [1. Marine animals.]   I. Title.   II. Series: Facts about (Austin, Tex.)
QL617.2.B33   1989
591'.92—dc20   89-2175
                                                CIP AC

Contents

Introduction	4	Hiding from Enemies	28
Simple Animals	6	Where Fish Live	30
Animals with Tentacles	8	Near the Coast	32
Mollusks	10	Coral Reefs	34
Octopuses and Squid	12	Deep-sea Fish	36
Crabs and Their Relatives	14	The Long Journeys	38
Starfish and Sea Urchins	16	Life in Fresh Water	40
What Is a Fish?	18	Freshwater Fish	42
Breathing and Moving	20	Water Animals in Danger	44
Fish Without Jaws	22		
Sharks and Rays	24	Glossary	46
Bony Fish	26	Index	48

Introduction

There are as many animals that live in water as there are on land. They live at all depths, but most water animals live near the surface.

The fish in our picture are salt-water fish living on a **coral reef** near the surface of the sea.

Other animals live far below the surface of the sea. Their bodies glow with tiny lights. Few of them grow to more than eight inches long.

Deep-sea fish sometimes look very fierce, like the one in our picture.

a deep-sea fish

krill

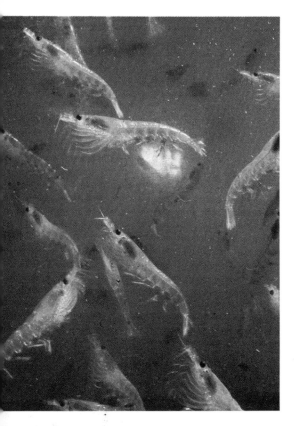

Many animals living in the sea feed on tiny animals called krill.

Krill look like tiny shrimps.

Their bodies are almost **transparent** and shine with light. They eat minute plants called **algae** that float in the water.

Fish, seals, whales, and birds eat krill.

5

Simple Animals

Our picture shows an **amoeba** which
is the simplest kind of animal.
Its body only has one **cell**
which is always changing shape.
The amoeba eats its food by
wrapping its cell body around it.
Amoebae live in ponds and lakes and
eat tiny plants.

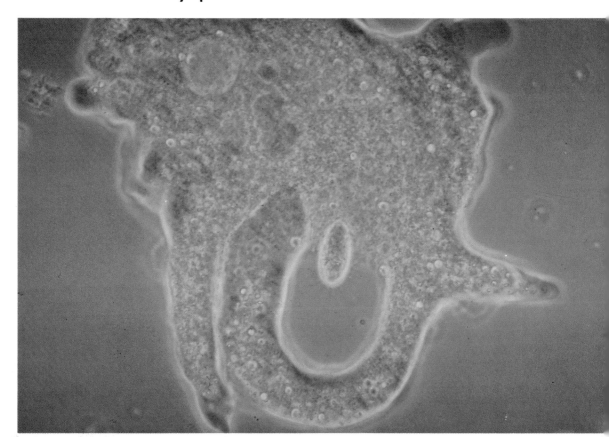

Plants and simple animals like sea shrimps are called **plankton** and are eaten by larger animals like fish.

Sponges are animals with many cells. They suck water and food in and out through the holes in their bodies.

sea shrimps

a group of sponges

Animals with Tentacles

Jellyfish live by the sea-shore and use their **tentacles** to look for food.

The thick tentacles are part of the jellyfish's mouth.

The thin tentacles are covered with stinging cells.

a jellyfish

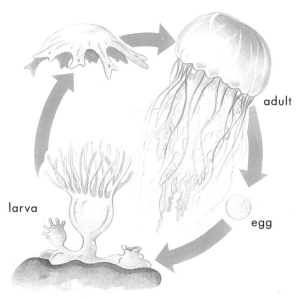

the life of a jellyfish

Jellyfish lay eggs that later turn into **larvae.**

The larvae attach themselves to the rocks and grow into young jellyfish. After several months the young jellyfish break free from the rock and float away.

8

Sea anemones live on rocks and look like flowers, but their "petals" are tentacles that they use to catch their food.

Our picture shows an anemone that has caught a fish.

When anemones are afraid, they pull their tentacles inside their bodies.

a sea anemone eating

these sea anemones are afraid

Mollusks

Snails, mussels, clams, and oysters are **mollusks** with hard chalky shells.

Clams have two halves to their shells and a powerful "foot" that they use to burrow into the sand or gravel. Giant clams are sometimes as big as three feet across.

The pearly nautilus is the only mollusk that can float.

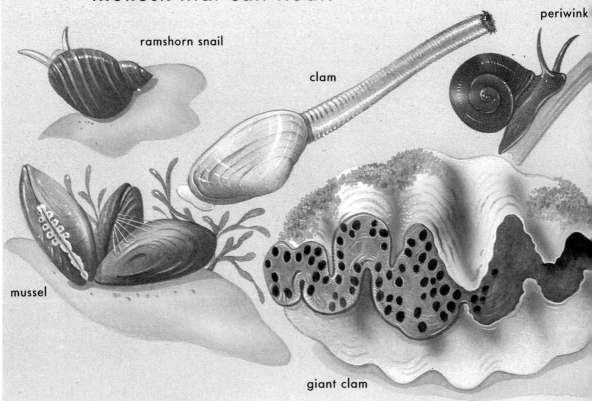

ramshorn snail

periwink

clam

mussel

giant clam

Mussels and oysters have **mother of pearl** inside their shells.

Whelks and limpets are sea snails; periwinkles and ramshorn snails are freshwater snails.

Although barnacles look like limpets, they are not mollusks, but relatives of crabs and shrimps.

pearly nautilus

whelk

limpet

oyster

barnacle

Octopuses and Squids

Octopuses and squids are mollusks,
but most of them don't have shells.
They swim by squirting water through
a tube, which pushes them along.
They also squirt a black "ink" to help
them escape from their enemies.

Octopuses and squids have tentacles
with suckers that cling to their prey.

Can you see the suckers of the octopus
in our picture?

a squid

a cuttlefish

Squids have eight short arms and two long arms that they use to catch fish.

A cuttlefish looks like a squid but has ten arms to look for food on the seabed. It can squirt ink like an octopus.

Crabs and Their Relatives

The fiddler crab has one claw that is larger than the other to attack its enemies.

Hermit crabs live in the empty shells of sea snails.

Sea anemones live on the shell of this crab. They help to protect it from its enemies.

a red fiddler crab

a hermit crab

Crabs, lobsters, shrimps, and prawns are all called **crustaceans.** They have hard outer shells to protect their bodies, and five pairs of legs. Some crustaceans live in fresh water, but most live in the sea.

Lobsters have longer bodies than crabs. They also have huge pincers to catch other animals.

Can you see the pincers on the lobster in our picture?

Starfish and Sea Urchins

Starfish usually have five arms. Under the arms are dozens of **tube-feet** that help the starfish to walk. If an enemy bites off an arm, the starfish can grow another one.

a cobalt starfish

underneath a starfish

Sea urchins live on the sand of the seabed and eat seaweed or small pieces of food.

They are covered with long sharp spines to protect them, which makes them look like round prickly balls. Sometimes the spines are hollow and have poison inside that the sea urchin injects into an enemy.

Other sea urchins have stinging tube-feet.

What Is a Fish?

Fish have **scales** on their bodies to protect them, and **fins** to help them swim. All fish have a long bony backbone and strong muscles for swimming.

The **swim bladder** helps the fish to move up or down in the water. The **gills** are used for breathing. The heart pumps blood around the body.

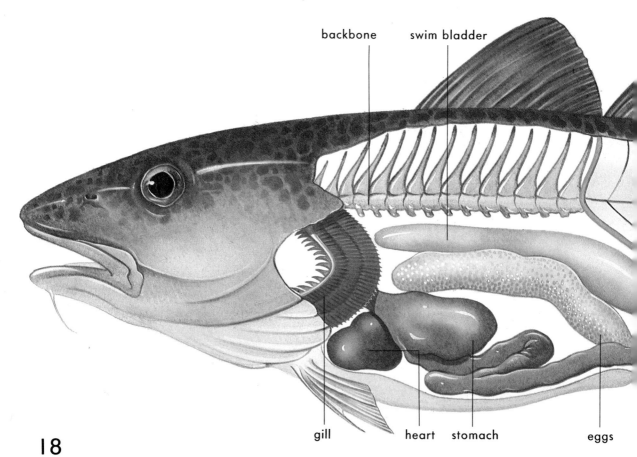

backbone   swim bladder

gill   heart   stomach   eggs

A codfish lays two or three million eggs which float near the surface of the water. The eggs hatch into baby fish called fry. The fry eat animals in the plankton.

Most fry are eaten by other animals but some survive to grow into adult fish.

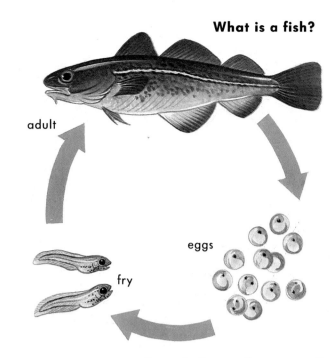

adult

eggs

fry

stages in the life of a cod

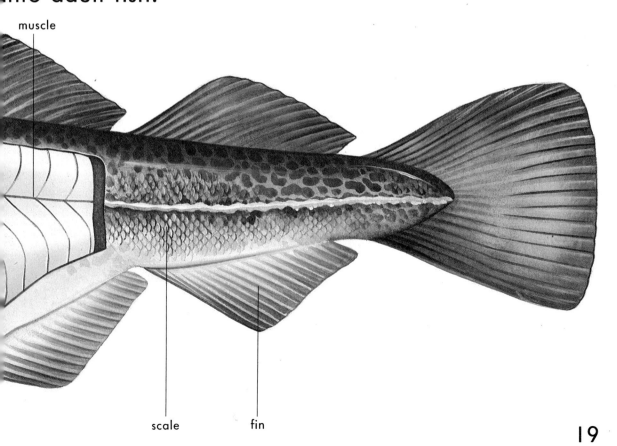

muscle

scale

fin

Breathing and Moving

Air and water both contain **oxygen,** which fish need to help turn their food into energy.

When fish breathe, they suck water into their mouths. Then the water is pumped from their mouths across their gills.

Blood flows through the gills and picks up the oxygen from the water.

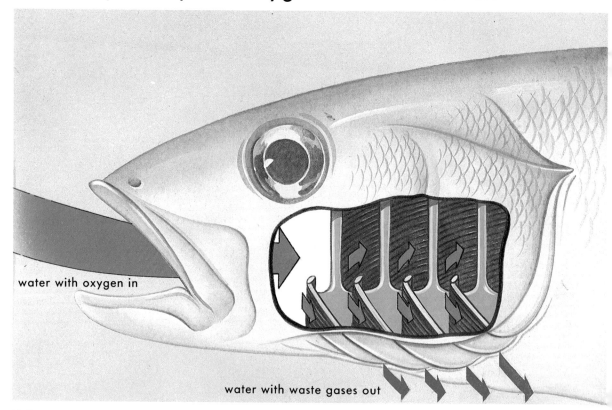

water with oxygen in

water with waste gases out

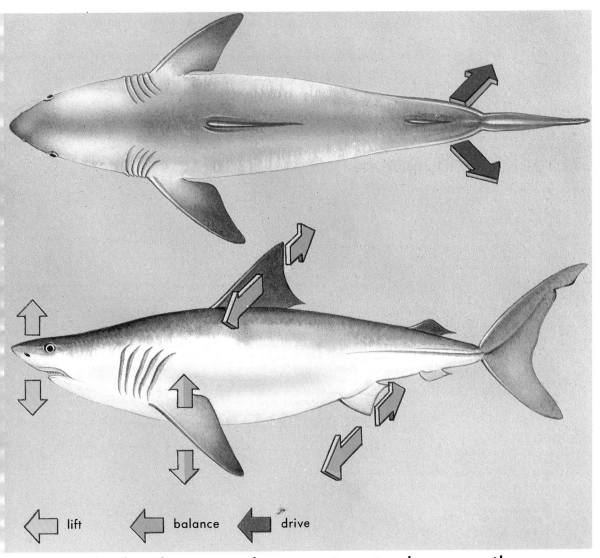

lift   balance   drive

A shark swims by moving its large tail from side to side. The large fin on its back and the fins beneath the body control the balance. The front fins and the shape of its head control the up and down movement.

A shark does not have a swim bladder. It must swim all the time or it will sink.

Fish Without Jaws

The fish that lived millions of years ago had no jaws.

These first fish fed on dead plants, which they sucked up because they could not bite.

Some jawless fish, like hagfish and lampreys, survive today. Hagfish live in deep oceans and because they have no fins or eyes, they use feelers around their mouths to find food.

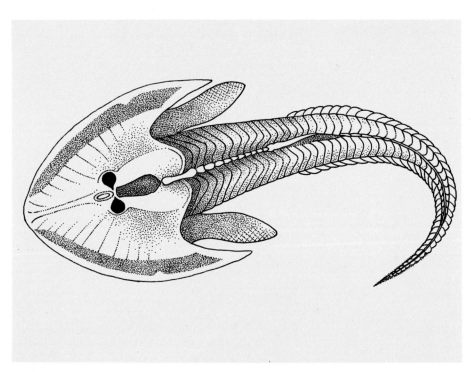

Pacific hagfish

A lamprey has eyes and fins and looks like an eel. It feeds by sucking blood from live fish.

Its mouth is a large sucker with horny teeth, which break the skin of a live fish so it bleeds.

The horny mouth of a lamprey

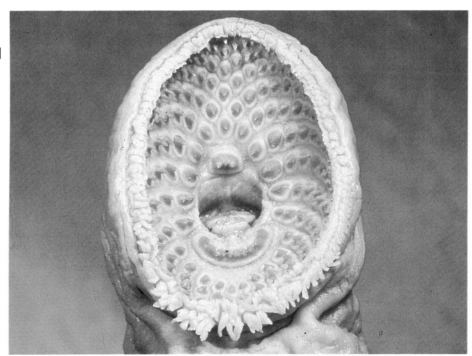

Sharks and Rays

A shark's mouth is under its head.
Most sharks have strong jaws.
The jaws carry rows of sharp teeth.
Sharks find their food by smell.
　Few sharks attack people, except
the great white shark, the hammerhead,
and the tiger shark in our picture, which
will attack anything that moves.

This bonnet shark follows trails of blood in the water and attacks wounded fish.

The electric ray in our picture below can produce a powerful electric shock that stuns its prey.

Bony Fish

A seahorse is a bony fish with a strange shape.

It swims slowly in an upright position.

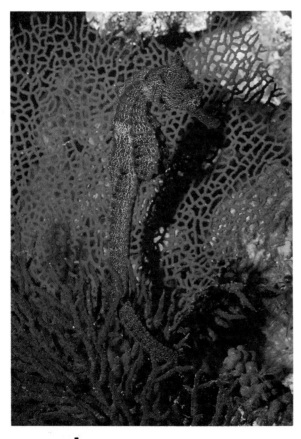

a seahorse

an angelfish

Most bony fish are long and rounded.

Some, like the angelfish, are flattened from side to side which helps them swim between plants. Others, like flounder, are flattened from top to bottom.

A few bony fish, like eels, are very long and thin.

The fish in our picture is a
coelacanth, which has not changed
its shape for millions of years.

It has a heavy body and thick scales,
which overlap for protection. It grows
up to four feet in length.

It feeds on other fish and lives in
deep water in rocky areas.

Its fins are unusual, as they are
thicker than the fins of other fish.

Hiding from Enemies

Fish have many enemies. Some fish use **camouflage** to hide from their enemies. The color and shape of the fish blends with its surroundings.

Camouflage not only helps the fish to hide from its enemies, but it also helps the fish to wait unseen for its prey to come close so that it can snap it up.

Can you see the well-camouflaged flounder in our picture?

n anglerfish

This anglerfish looks like rock covered with weeds.

Porcupine fish protect themselves with spines.

If the porcupine fish is attacked, it puffs out its body so that the spines stick out.

a porcupine fish

Where Fish Live

Our picture shows that fish live at different layers in the oceans, but most live near the surface.

surface layer

food sinks to ocean floor

ocean floor

These fish feed on plants and other animals near the surface.

Our map shows that the deepest water in the world is in the four oceans. The water at the bottom of the oceans is dark and cold. No light comes down from the surface, so the fish that live down there are often blind.

These fish live on the dead plants and animals that sink down to the ocean floor from the surface.

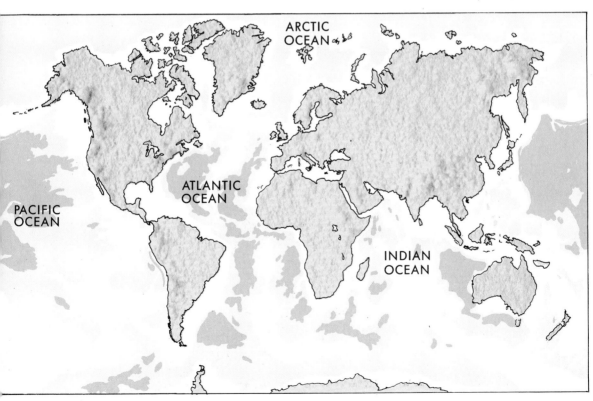

ARCTIC OCEAN

ATLANTIC OCEAN

PACIFIC OCEAN

INDIAN OCEAN

Near the Coast

Many plants, animals, and fish live
in the sea near the coast.
Flounder are well camouflaged for life
on the seabed.

a shoal of bream

a flounder on the seabed

Huge numbers of fish live in the warm shallow waters near the coast. They eat snails or small shrimps. Herring and bream swim about in **shoals.**

The brightly colored wrasse in our picture lives near the seabed.

Sole, flounders, and halibut live on sandy seabeds. They are all flatfish, with eyes on top of their heads, so that they can watch out for food above them.

Coral Reefs

When a **volcano** is thrust up from the seabed, it is worn away in thousands of years to leave a ring-shaped island. Coral grows in the warm shallow seas, to form a reef around the island.

coral

Corals are small animals that live
close together in chalky tubes.
When the animals die, the chalky tubes
remain and form a type of rock
called coral.

A coral reef is home to many animals.
Our picture shows sea anemones waiting
to trap small fish in their tentacles.

A clown fish lives near the anemones.
It helps keep the anemones clean by
eating the small pieces of food that
get trapped between the tentacles.

Deep-sea Fish

Most deep-sea fish live in the mud on the ocean floor. Some feed on the mud itself, which is rich in dead bodies.

Most deep-sea fish are colored red or black, but a few are clear like glass.

Almost all of these fish have huge gaping mouths and large teeth.

Some glow in the dark, like the lantern fish. It has rows of tiny lights along its body.

a lantern fish

Deep-sea anglerfish live 11,500 feet down. They have sharp teeth and glowing **lures** that dangle from their mouths to attract their prey.

a deep-sea anglerfish

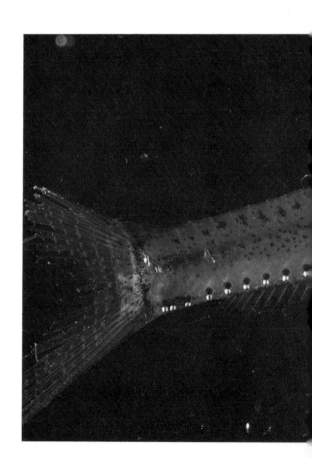

The Long Journeys

Adult salmon live in the sea. In the autumn they return to the river where they were born. The female salmon makes a nest in the gravel. Then she lays thousands of eggs. The eggs hatch and the babies, called **parr,** live in the river for three years. When the parr are four inches long they swim to the sea and are now called **smolts.** The smolts grow quickly and reach 28 inches long and become adult salmon.

an Atlantic eel

where eels breed

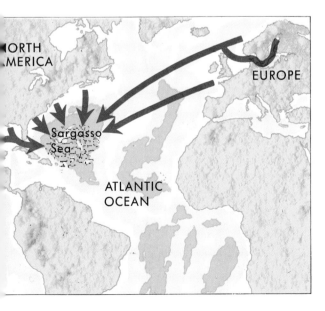

NORTH
AMERICA

EUROPE

Sargasso
Sea

ATLANTIC
OCEAN

Eels live in fresh water and travel to lay their eggs in the Sargasso Sea. The baby eels are carried by the **currents** to the river mouths. The young eels, called **elvers,** swim up the rivers to become adult eels.

Life in Fresh Water

Many animals live in fresh water.

This pond snail lives in fresh water. It comes up to the surface of the pond to breathe.

a pond snail

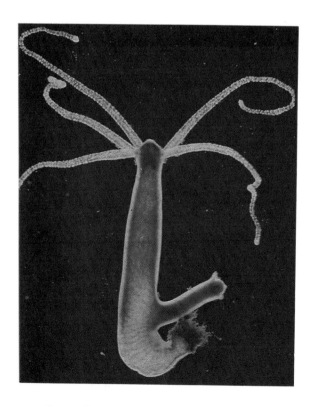

a hydra

Hydras have simple bodies and tentacles that are armed with stinging darts. These are used to kill the tiny animals that the hydra eats.

Hydras breed by growing "buds" that break away to form new hydras.

You can see a bud growing on the hydra in our picture.

The water beetle in our picture is carrying a bubble of air with it so that it can breathe while underwater.

Many freshwater animals find life very difficult in streams and ponds. Many ponds dry out in the summer. In fast-moving streams they have to cling on hard so they won't get swept away. Most of these animals live under stones or in the gravel.

Freshwater Fish

Freshwater fish come in all sorts of shapes and sizes. The largest is the sturgeon, which can grow to over 18 feet in length. The shape of a fish tells us about where it lives and how it gets food.

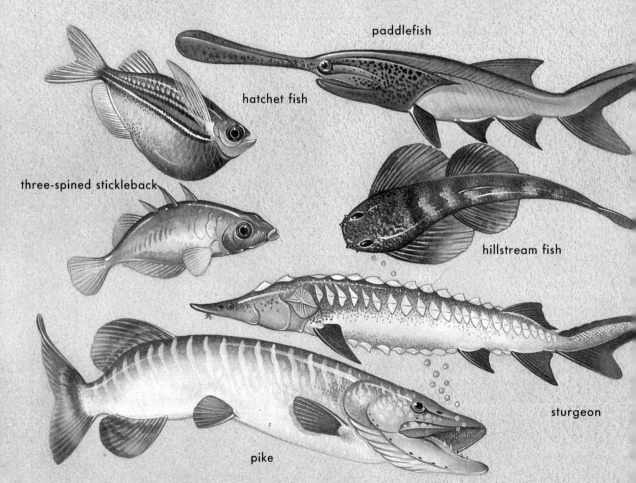

paddlefish

hatchet fish

three-spined stickleback

hillstream fish

sturgeon

pike

Paddlefish and sturgeon have long
noses to find prey in muddy riverbeds.
Catfish use their whiskers, or **barbels,**
to feel for food in the mud.

Hatchet fish have upturned mouths
to feed at the surface of the water.

The long, thin bodies of gar and
pike help them to swim among weed
beds. Pike eat other small fish.

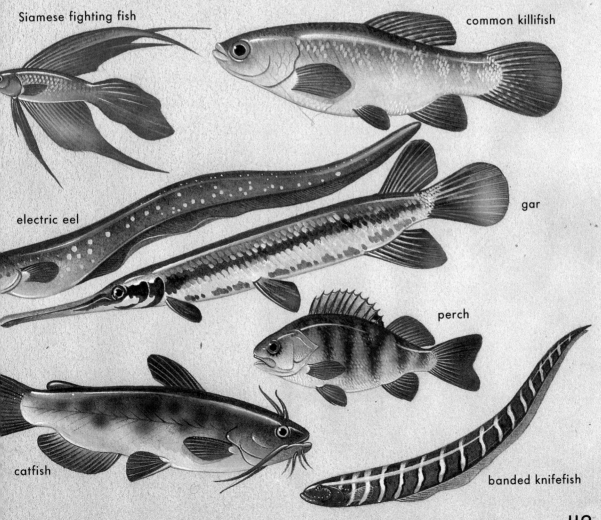

Siamese fighting fish

common killifish

electric eel

gar

perch

catfish

banded knifefish

Water Animals in Danger

Our picture shows a dead rainbow trout floating upside down in a river.

The river water has been **polluted** so all the plants, animals, and fish have died. This fish has been killed by poisonous **chemicals** that were dumped into the river.

an oil slick

algae

Other chemicals make masses of
algae grow, which choke up the rivers
and use all the oxygen in the water so
all the other plants and animals die.
The sea also is often polluted by oil
which kills the fish and sea birds.

Glossary

algae   very simple plants. Algae do not have roots, leaves, or flowers. They are usually tiny and can be green, red, or brown.

amoeba   a tiny animal. An amoeba changes its shape all the time and lives in water.

barbel   a thick "hair" that sticks out from the mouth of some fish. Fish use their barbels to find food in the mud.

camouflage   the colors or shapes of an animal's body that help it to hide in its surroundings.

cell   a very small unit of living matter. Most animals are made up of millions of cells.

chemicals   used to spray crops and fields to kill insects, to make crops grow well, and to control weeds and fungus diseases.

coral reef   a wall of hard "rock" built up of dead corals in shallow seas.

crustacean   a type of water animal that has a hard shell.

currents   the flow of water within a sea, lake, or river.

elver   a young eel.

fin   a flat piece of skin and bone attached to the side or back of a fish. Fish use their fins to steer their bodies through the water.

gill   a part of a water animal used for breathing under water. Most animals with gills cannot breathe out of the water.

larva   a young stage in the life of certain animals. Larvae look different from the adults.

lure   something that one animal uses to attract another animal.

mollusk   an animal with a soft body that usually lives in a shell. Snails, oysters, and clams are mollusks.

mother of pearl   a hard silvery material found on the inside of mollusk shells. Oysters and mussels surround grains of sand that enter their shells with mother of pearl. The result is a beautiful natural pearl.

oxygen   a gas found in the air and in water, which an animal needs for breathing.

parr   a baby salmon.

plankton   tiny plants and animals that float near the surface of the seas, oceans, and inland waters. Plankton is a source of food for many water animals.

polluted   spoiled or made unclean by chemicals and waste matter.

scale   a small flat thin ''plate'' found on the skin of fish. Scales are made of a hard material to protect the soft body of the fish.

shoal   a large group of fish swimming together.

smolt   a young stage in the life of a salmon, when it travels from the river to the sea.

sponge   the simplest kind of water animal with many cells. It has a soft body that is full of holes so it can take in water easily. Sponges do not move.

swim bladder   a part of a fish's body that can be filled with air. The swim bladder keeps a fish from sinking.

tentacle   a long arm, or feeler, of an animal. Tentacles are used for feeling, holding, moving, or stinging.

transparent   something that you can see through.

tube-feet   tiny ''suckers'' used by sea urchins and starfish to move, and grip food.

volcano   a hole in the Earth's crust through which molten rock and ash are forced from deep inside the Earth to the surface. The outflowing lava and ash make a cone that grows higher and higher until a mountain is formed with a hole or crater in the middle.

Index

algae 5, 45
amoeba 6
angelfish 26
anglerfish 29, 36

barbels 43
barnacles 11
bream 32, 33

camouflage 28
catfish 43
clams 10
clown fish 35
cod 19
coelacanth 27
coral reef 4, 34, 35
crabs 11, 14, 15
crustaceans 15
cuttlefish 13

eels 26, 39
eggs 8, 19, 38, 39
electric ray 25
elvers 39

fins 18, 21, 22, 23, 27

flatfish 33
flounder 26, 28, 33
fry 19

gar 43
gills 18, 20

hagfish 22
halibut 33
hatchet fish 43
herring 33
hydra 40

jellyfish 8

krill 5

lamprey 22, 23
lantern fish 36
limpets 11
lobsters 15
lures 36

mollusks 10, 11, 12
mother of pearl 11
mussels 10, 11

octopus 12
oysters 10, 11

paddlefish 43
pearly nautilus 10
periwinkles 11

pike 43
plankton 7, 19
porcupine fish 29
prehistoric fish 22

rainbow trout 44

salmon 38
Sargasso Sea 39
scales 18, 27
sea anemones 9, 14, 35
seahorse 26
sea urchins 17
sharks 24, 25
shrimps 7, 11, 15, 33
smolts 38
snails 11, 14, 33, 40
sole 33
sponges 7
squid 12, 13
starfish 16
sturgeon 42, 43
swim bladder 18, 21

teeth 23, 24, 36
tentacles 8, 9, 12, 35, 4

water beetle 41
whelks 11
wrasse 33

Photographic credits (t=top b=bottom l=left r=right) Cover photograph Anthony Bannister/NHPA; title page Frank Lane Picture Agency; 4 Warren Williams/Seaphot; 5t Peter David/Seaphot; 5b Peter Johnson/NHPA; 6 M.I. Walker/NHPA; 7t Peter David/Seaphot; 7b Pete Atkinson/Seaphot; 8t Peter Vine/Seaphot; 9t Alex Kerstitch/Seaphot; 9b M.D. Griffiths/Seaphot; 12 Alex Kerstitch/Seaphot 13t Peter David/Seaphot; 13b Herwarth Voigtmann/Seaphot; 14t David Maitland/Seaphot; 14b David George/Seaphot; 15 Alex Kerstitch/Seaphot; 16t Richard Chesher/Seaphot; 16b Anthony Bannister/NHPA; 17 Mick Laverack/Seaphot;23t, 23b Ken Lucas/Seaphot; 24 Christian Petron/Seaphot; 25t Ken Lucas/Seaphot; 25b Roy Manstan/Seaphot; 26t Richard Chester/Seaphot; 26b Alex Kerstitch/Seaphot; 27 Peter Scoones/Seaphot; 28 C.S. Milkins/Aquila; 29t Jim Greenfield/Seaphot; 29b Christian Petron/Seaphot; 32t Peter Scoones/Seaphot; 32b Geoff Harwood/Seaphot; 33 Peter Scoones/Seaphot; 34t Warren Williams/Seaphot; 35 Herwarth Voigtman/Seaphot; 36/37, 37t Peter David/Seaphot; 38 Gilbert van Ryckevorsel/Seaphot; 39t John and Gillian Lythgoe/Seaphot; 40t G.I. Bernard/NHPA; 40b M. Walker/NHPA; 41 Steve Nicholls/Seaphot; 44 Chris Howes/Seaphot; 45t Warren Williams/Seaphot; 45b G.I. Bernard/NHPA.